Luigi Pirandello

by OLGA RAGUSA

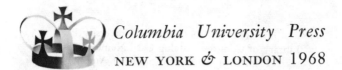 Columbia University Press

NEW YORK & LONDON 1968

COLUMBIA ESSAYS ON MODERN WRITERS is a series of critical studies of English, Continental, and other writers whose works are of contemporary artistic and intellectual significance.

Editor: William York Tindall

Advisory Editors

Jacques Barzun   W. T. H. Jackson   Joseph A. Mazzeo   Justin O'Brien

Luigi Pirandello is Number 37 of the series

OLGA RAGUSA is Professor of Italian at Columbia University. She is the author of *Mallarmé in Italy* and *Verga's Milanese Tales.*

Copyright © 1968 Columbia University Press
Library of Congress Catalog Card Number: 68–54457
Printed in the United States of America

By permission of the Pirandello Estate passages from the works of Pirandello are quoted in the author's own translation from the Mondadori edition of *Tutti i romanzi* and *Maschere nude.*

Luigi Pirandello

Pirandello belongs to the constellation of European writers who in the early part of the century were concerned with fixing the dimensions of the human condition—Proust, Joyce, Kafka, Musil, Thomas Mann. His stature has been diminished by his having been assigned almost exclusively to the history of the theatre. His message has been deformed in an abstract formulation of his thought which effectively reduces the *portée* of his art.

In Pirandello criticism it is customary to gloss over his naturalistic beginnings and hasten to the more characteristic works which have turned his name into an adjective descriptive of an epoch. Of seven novels, two hundred and fifty short stories, forty-four plays, and a fat volume of essays, poems, occasional writings, and fragments, only three or four plays—not to limit the number even further to the two anthology pieces, *Six Characters in Search of an Author* and *Henry IV*—are generally known and discussed. It is true that these are equally familiar in France and in Germany, in the United States and in England, in Spain and in Sweden—indeed, wherever there has been an avant-garde theatre. Pirandello shares with a small number of other writers the privilege of being prized independently of the tradition from which he stems. Not as an Italian but as a European writer did he leave his mark on the modern theatre.

Pirandello was born in 1867 during a cholera epidemic in which there were more than 50,000 deaths. His mother had been forced to leave Girgenti and seek refuge a few miles farther west along Sicily's southern coast, at the family's farm-house, situated in a region known as Caos. These circumstances later permitted Pirandello to write with his wonted talent for effect: "I am, then, the child of Chaos."

Girgenti, or Agrigento, to give it the ancient name which was restored to it in 1927, is the Greek city of Akragas, destroyed by the Carthaginians, conquered by the Romans, and in the ninth century fallen prey to the Arabs. Of all Sicily, the region of Agrigento continues even today to bear the deepest imprint of Arabic culture, "that sense of violence, that presence of sinister and mysterious forces," in the words of Mack Smith. In his historical novel, *The Old and the Young* (1908), Pirandello was to recall Girgenti's streets and its unhappy inhabitants: the narrow, slippery, ill-smelling alleys; the women seated on their doorsteps day in day out; the dark, guttural sounds of their speech broken by the long, emphatic interjections; the bashful, troubled anxiety of their frightened and flashing eyes; the city's many idlers walking up and down the main street, with un-changing step, drowned in boredom, automatons and not living beings. "The Akragas of the Greeks, the Agrigentum of the Romans, had ended up in the Kerkent of the Mohammedans, and the mark of the Arabs had remained indelible in the souls and customs of the people. Taciturn apathy, suspicious mistrust, and jealousy." Essentially the Arabic heritage meant a rigidly formal and immobile social structure, with its accompanying sense of reticence and secretiveness, its private language full of allusions instead of open statements, and the blocking of the individual's psyche, with the perennial danger of a sudden and irremediable explosion. The conflict between self and role which was to play such an important part in Pirandello's figura-tion of the human condition appears here for the first time as an element of his experience.

Other facts relative to Girgenti must be borne in mind for

an understanding of Pirandello. His family, on both sides, had been deeply involved in the struggle for Sicilian independence from the Bourbons and in Garibaldi's campaign for the liberation of southern Italy. The political feelings of the Ricci Gramittos (the mother's family) and the Pirandellos were, however, quite different in origin. The former, a family of professional men of Porto Empedocle (Girgenti's industrial district), had already incurred the ire of the government in 1848, and Pirandello's grandfather, a combative lawyer of separatist convictions, had had to join other exiles in Malta, where he died young, a victim of Bourbon oppression. The Pirandellos, on the other hand, had come from Liguria in the mid-1700s. They were businessmen, trading in the characteristic Sicilian products, citrus fruits and sulphur. When Stefano joined Garibaldi in 1860, and then again in 1862, it was more out of a feeling of adventure and later of personal gratitude to the General who had saved his life in a skirmish, than because of any tradition of political action or idealism such as had directed the Ricci Gramittos. Stefano Pirandello was an active, practical man. At the time of Luigi's birth, he was busy overseeing the sulphur mines his oldest brother had rented and was working at Porto Empedocle. Overseeing meant also, occasionally, to clash with the powerful sulphur mafia, to shoot and be shot at. Memories of the hopeful and passionate days of the Risorgimento, whose elegy Pirandello was to write in *The Old and the Young*, were kept alive by the mother rather than the father—one indication, among many more dramatic ones, of a divergence in temperament as well as background within a typically tense family situation in which the authoritarian and irascible *paterfamilias* virtually terrorizes the others into submission.

Pirandello was to have the opportunity to become acquainted at firsthand with the environment of his father's activities when he spent the summer of 1886 working with him at Porto

Empedocle. Again, *The Old and the Young* is a good source for an impression of the intolerable realities of life at Porto Empedocle, under the harsh rays of the southern sun: the continuous creaking of the loaded lorries, the endless confusion of barefoot men and of beasts of burden, the open sewers on the beach, men standing waist-deep in water and yet dying of thirst. "No one cares; no one complains. They all seem to have gone mad down there, turned into animals by the mean, ferocious fight for gain!" Pirandello's encounter with the struggle for economic survival in the sulphur industry was to leave its traces in his work, especially in a number of short stories of which "Fumes" (1901) shows the greatest familiarity with documentary detail and "Ciàula scopre la luna" (1912) is the most powerful. But in practical terms Pirandello's effort to follow in his father's footsteps was to end in failure, showing him his fundamental incapacity to join in this aspect of men's lives. Gaspare Giudice, Pirandello's recent biographer, has seen with great sensitivity how much of Pirandello himself has gone into the figure of the protagonist of another short story, "Lontano" (1901). Lars Cleen is a Norwegian sailor brought ashore ill with typhus, who recuperates under the care of the Scandinavian vice-consul at Porto Empedocle (one of Pirandello's most marvelously grotesque figures) and marries his niece. An exile in a, to him, strange, incomprehensible, and repellent land, he becomes an object of scorn to the natives. Pirandello describes him in a magnificent image of alienation: "He . . . would sit on the low wall of the pier and watch the ships at anchor. . . . People would stop to stare at him in his half-bewildered, half-enraptured attitude: they looked at him as though he were a crane or a stork, tired and lost, that had descended from the heights of the sky."

At the end of the summer Pirandello returned to Palermo, where a few months before he had completed his secondary ed-

ucation, and became a law student at the University. The choice
of subject matter was, of course, the father's, for Pirandello had
already in his teens showed a preference for literary studies. He
had also begun to write poetry; two manuscript notebooks go
back to 1883. Pirandello's career as a law student was short-
lived, and with an excuse he obtained his father's permission to
transfer to the University of Rome. At Rome he was not a more
successful student. Though he at once abandoned the study of
law, he found his professors of literature far from inspiring. A
classroom episode eventually led to his expulsion, and to his
moving in 1889 to the University of Bonn. The reasons for
Pirandello's sojourn at a German university have often been
stated erroneously. He did not go to Germany to study philos-
ophy, although his familiar juxtapositions of appearance and
reality gave that impression to some of his more superficial critics. Pirandello was advised by the only one of his Rome professors who had taken an interest in him to go to Bonn in order
to pursue his studies in the new field of Romance Philology at
the very place where the great scholar Friedrich Diez had
founded that discipline. This also explains the choice of his
dissertation topic. He wrote on his native dialect of the province
of Girgenti, not from provincialism or nostalgia, but because it
was a good philological subject on which he could be presumed
to have firsthand data.

A number of articles that Pirandello contributed to a Floren-
tine periodical while in Bonn are further proof of the nature of
his interests at the time. One was the result of a trip to Cologne,
where the young scholar recalled the much more famous visit
of his predecessor Petrarch, taking the occasion to compare the
rich flowering of German studies on Humanism and the Renais-
sance with the meager and unmethodical work being done on
the same subject in Italy. Another one was suggested by his
reading of Verga's *Mastro don Gesualdo*, but it is a disappoint-

ment to find that it deals not with the novel but with the habitual uneasiness of the Italian writer faced by a traditional and static literary language that inhibits spontaneity and inventiveness. Of special significance is his work in progress: a series of studies on three comic writers, humorists, of the Duecento, the poets Cecco Angiolieri, Folgore di San Gimignano, and Cene della Chitarra. This point is important, for it underlines the fact that even the theoretical essay *L'umorismo* (1908), the cornerstone statement of Pirandello's art, owes its origin to his positivistic, philological training—a fact often obscured when the chronology of Pirandello's writings is lost sight of, or when excerpts are translated out of context (as in the parts of the essay available in English), in the belief that the essence of the author's thought can be captured without heeding the examples that illustrate it. But, like every poet, Pirandello deals with the concrete. His definition of humor is no more thinkable without the long historical excursus on the semantics of the word and the review of Italian humorists that precedes it than the parable *It is So!* (*If You Think So*) (1917) would be complete without the veiled figure of Signora Ponza who appears at the end, in all her palpable blackness, to bring the action to its resolution.

The essay on humor and a volume of collected studies, *Arte e scienza*, were published in 1908, at a time when Pirandello was competing for a permanent appointment as Professor of Italian at the Normal School in Rome. His early days in Rome, after his return from Germany, had been carefree and devoted to literature. It was only after 1903 that his activity as a writer passed from enjoyable dilettantism to necessary professionalism. The first product of the new pressures was a novel of great success, *The Late Mattia Pascal* (1904), which was written serially, thought up month by month, dependent on the free, spontaneous flow of the imagination. In Pirandello's own terminology, it is an example of subjective as opposed to objective narration, a psychological rather than a naturalistic work.

With 1904 we are on the threshold of the most important period in the development of Pirandello's personality as a writer. Biographical facts cease to matter. Pirandello becomes more and more simply "a man who writes." As he was to say in an autobiographical note published in a Rome periodical in 1924, "There is nothing noteworthy in my life. It is a completely inner life, concentrated in my work and in my thoughts which . . . are far from cheerful." And even more inclusively in a statement made in 1921, "Our imagination and our intelligence are nourished by knowledge and sense impressions up to a certain age; afterwards, nothing further reaches us from the outside that the mind by itself is incapable of intuiting and creating."

The history of Pirandello's external success has its high points in a number of epoch-making performances of his plays. His work thus became known first through drama reviews and the daily press, and this origin of his reputation has colored all subsequent efforts to analyze and assess the multiple aspects of his production. I speak of this because, as with all stirring and controversial writers—writers who continue to be contemporary after their day—it is often difficult to separate Pirandello from the widely repeated generalizations about his work. Moreover, a glance at the Bibliography at the end of this essay will show how little of Pirandello's work is readily available in English and how heavily what there is relates to the theatre; the situation for other languages is not essentially different. In Italy, too, Pirandello first attracted notice through the theatre, but his *succès de scandale* in that area was quite early (1923) curbed and given the stamp of respectability by Adriano Tilgher's seminal formulation of the clash between Life and Form (move-

[9]

ment and rigidity, face and mask, reality and fiction) as the basic concept of his vision. Thematic criticism, once set rolling, naturally tended to seek supporting material from the writer's total output and led to such works as Janner's *Luigi Pirandello* (1948), nine tenths of which is devoted to the short stories and the novels. Beginning with Antonio Di Pietro's magnificent and unjustly overlooked *Saggio su Luigi Pirandello* (1941), all serious work on Pirandello has aimed at giving the complete story of his development.

It is my conviction that he deserves no less than that. Not simply because we owe that kind of attention to any writer of his stature, but because it is arbitrary in his case to separate the narrative from the dramatic worlds—a procedure which, given the strong links in characters, plot, and themes between the two, would be understandable only if we were interested solely in rhetorical or purely formal criticism. Furthermore, there is in Pirandello no clear break between the manner in which he himself experienced the world and the manner in which his fictional figures experience it. Not that Pirandello's work is autobiographical in the ordinary sense of being the direct transposition of life into art: all attempts to read him in that light— his wife's mental illness and his adherence to fascism being the principal stumbling blocks—fall lamentably into the ridiculous. But Pirandello is a highly subjective writer who projects his feelings on everything he touches. In the Preface to *Six Characters* (1925), he makes a fundamental distinction between two kinds of writers, those who are satisfied with representing figures, narrating events, or describing landscapes for the sheer pleasure of doing so, and those others—among whom he places himself—who have a deeper spiritual need and will consider figures, events, or landscapes only if they are "imbued with a particular sense of life" which gives them universal value. The first of these he calls historical writers, the second philosophical.

I would propose instead the designation realists and moralists, bearing in mind that insofar as he is a moralist Pirandello is naturally also a realist (the moralist's insights being the result of observation and experience), but that insofar as he is an artist he is not a realist because with the moralist's single-mindedness he pursues meaning and rejects surface. It goes without saying that by moralist I do not mean the narrowly prescriptive dictator of rules of conduct. In terms of nineteenth-century literary movements, Pirandello is thus not a naturalist, because he shuns naturalism's scientific approach—its programmatic objectivity and impersonality—in favor of a kind of absolute involvement on the part of the writer. This obliterates all distance between himself and the characters he creates, and goes so far as to involve even the reader in the creation of the work, so that on stage, eventually, the traditional removal of audience from represented fictional world will be wiped out.

The uncompromising rage that drives Pirandello to unmask man's cruelty to man is the moralist's horrified reaction at finding an unbridgeable abyss between things as they are and things as they should be. In the formulation of his poetics, the concept of the comic—the awareness of the incongruous (*avvertimento del contrario*)—and the concept of humor—the sense of the incongruous (*sentimento del contrario*)—are respectively the realistic and the moralistic (or idealistic) moments, the perception of the phenomenon and the transcendence of it. Man's cruelty finds its fullest expression not in uncontrolled psychological forces (anarchistic sadism) but in social institutions and restraints, whether these take the form of the invasion of privacy which the Ponzas must suffer in *It is So!* in order to assure the family's breadwinner continued employment, or whether they cause the psychological immobilization, the deprivation of inner life to which the nameless protagonist of *When One Is Somebody* (1933) is condemned because his admiring public will not accept any change in his image. It is important to emphasize that Pirandello's alienated protagonist, his man on the brink of madness, does not, for all his frenetic activity and suffering, resort to crime. Ciampa, for instance, in *Il berretto a sonagli* (1917), does everything he can to avoid an irreparable act, and if the nameless protagonist of *Henry IV* (1922) kills, he immediately punishes himself by turning his back on the social world and accepting his exclusion from it as definitive. In Pirandello, then, alienation forces man to come to firmer grips with himself, to create new values; his self-assertion is achieved through renunciation. Thus the staid, respected lawyer in "La carriola" (1916?) guards against an impulse to madness, against the wild surge of irresponsibility, by allowing himself each day one carefully dosed-out moment of irrationality: when he is sure that no one is about, he tiptoes to lock the door of his office and with a "fearful joy" in which with trembling he recognizes "the voluptuousness of a divine, self-aware insanity" and which for an instant recompenses him for the hated role he is condemned to play in life, as though he were a naughty child he picks up the hind paws of his dog and holding them forces it to walk around on its front paws. Belluca, the accountant in "Il treno ha fischiato" (1914), the type of clerk Gogol and Dostoyevsky have rendered immortal, has been enslaved by an impossible home situation so that he is now like "an old donkey with blinders on its eyes, pulling its cart quietly and evenly, always along the same road." Then one night he hears the whistle of a train, and suddenly, as when he was young, the whole world opens up before him with its magic cities, known and unknown, its lands, mountains, forests, seas . . . At work the next day, strong in his new-found freedom, he rebels against the manager, bursts into senseless fury, and is taken to the hospital. His stay there is brief, his recovery rapid, but on condition that he can keep his private safety-valve, insisting henceforth on the right to escape from time to time, "between one column of figures and the next, to Siberia . . . or . . . to the forests of the Congo." To call experiences such as these frustration rather than ascetic reconciliation, a self-imposed catharsis, is to ignore or misunderstand the great ethical tradition of Western civilization and Pirandello's place in it.

When we consider him as essentially a moralist—that is, when we consider him in his totality—it becomes strongly evident that Pirandello belongs chronologically and intellectually to the declining years of the nineteenth century. The theory of Romanticism that Morse Peckham has in recent years evolved seems particularly well suited to serve as the broad outline against which Pirandello can best be viewed. Peckham covers all aspects of the movement, presenting the "Romantic problem" in metaphysical, emotional, social, and epistemological terms. As he puts it, in Romanticism "the transcendence of phenomena became an indivisible aspect of the encounter with phenomena" (and we have mentioned how this is true in Pirandello's theory of humor); the sense of value was sought "in the psychological fact that men can and must create a sense of value" (and we have seen how this works in Pirandello's solution to alienation); the personality was divided internally "by distinguishing and separating the self from the role" (and we need hardly point out how this is one of Pirandello's basic intuitions); and "perception and cognition were seen as under the control of the will" (and here I would make a distinction between the manner in which Pirandello himself perceived the world and the manner in which some—though not all—of his characters do). In his innumerable case histories, Pirandello portrays over and over again the plight of Romantic man suffering the breakdown of certainties and forced to come to terms with his fragmented personality, his social and metaphysical solitude. The situation is represented emblematically, with rare force, in a passage of

[13]

The Late Mattia Pascal which makes use of theatre imagery but is really about the spiritual condition of contemporary man. The announcement is made that an adaptation of Sophocles' *Electra* is to be played in a marionette theatre:

—The tragedy of Orestes?
—Exactly! . . . But listen to the strange idea I've had! What would happen if at the climax, when the marionette playing Orestes is about to avenge the death of his father, if at that very moment the paper sky of the theatre would be rent apart? . . . Orestes would be terribly disconcerted by that hole in the sky . . . he would continue to feel the impulse to punish, he would want to follow through with passionate action, but his eyes would move to that tear and remain fixed there. . . . In brief, Orestes would turn into Hamlet. The whole difference, signor Meis, between ancient and modern tragedy lies in that hole in a paper sky.

. . .

Happy are the marionettes, I thought to myself, above whose wooden heads the artificial sky remains unbroken! . . . And they can go about their business bravely and enjoy the comedy they are playing, and love and hold themselves in high esteem, without ever feeling dizzy or faint, for that sky is a roof of the right proportions for their size and their actions.

What is striking here is not so much a felicitous but incidental formulation of the difference between ancient and modern tragedy, as the identification of man with the puppet, his diminution in stature from free agent to helpless object, his reduction to mechanical automatism. To see man in this perspective, no longer king in his palace but, as Pirandello wrote to a sister in 1886, spider in its web, snail in its shell, mollusk in its conch, and to see the world from sidereal distances so that, as he wrote in another letter in 1887, it shrinks to the size of a lemon, is typical of Pirandello's existential despair and its concrete poetic expression. An important article, "Arte e coscienza d'oggi" (1893), ties these subjective apprehensions to the contemporary cultural situation. Positivism, Pirandello writes, has explained the universe as a living machine and has established man's place in nature—a melancholy place indeed, in comparison to the one he had earlier imagined: "This poor earth of ours! An incommensurably small atom in space, a cheap little top one day hurled off by the sun and ever since circling it on its immutable path. What has man become? This microcosm, this king of the universe? Alas, poor man! Can't you just see King Lear, armed with a broomstick, jump in front of you, in all his tragic comicality? What is he raving about?" In the very deepest sense, all of Pirandello's works will be a representation of that raving and an answer to that question.

Mattia Pascal is the first major character created by Pirandello, but he does not belong to the group of more famous characters, those "without author." And he is not a Lear set raving on the stage. In the second part of the book, while he lives the extraordinary and exhilarating adventure of a man whom chance has permitted to escape from the binding determinants of life, he is the typical "voyageur sans bagage," the "stranger in life," and in this sense the happy prefiguration of what will later turn into the tragic protagonist of *Henry IV*. Because of the essential gaiety of *The Late Mattia Pascal*, it is perhaps not easy to see at once the kinship between the nameless Emperor whose mask hides no face, and the small-town librarian, momentarily so rich in *disponibilité* that he can create his own personality, choose a name and a background, a place of birth and an education, his occupation and his leisure with the same freedom, the same poetic license with which Pirandello himself sets out to mold his characters. Of course, there is disgust, rebellion, and hate at the core of Mattia's experience. He runs away from home because he has been the victim of fraud and stupidity, of the overriding egotism of his mother-in-law, and because death has deprived him of the only two beings he loved, his mother and his infant daughter. There is also great sadness in the defeat of his dream of freedom, a defeat that builds up step by step, inexorably, and culminates in his willing acceptance of the very institutions he had first anarchistically denied. The moments of growing self-knowledge in Adriano Meis, Mattia's new "I," are small epiphanies, episodes of the plot treated by Pirandello with a unique mixture of amusement and pathos: Adriano realizes that without an *état civil* he cannot own a puppy which must be registered, that for fear of his being unmasked his conversation with his fellow men is limited to the most superficial banalities, that he must not fall in love with a trusting, innocent girl unless he is ready to run the risk of hurting her, that he cannot bring the man who robbed him to justice, nor challenge the man who insulted him to a duel. He is immobilized, frozen in his non-being, in his "life after death," as effectively as he had been in the coercion and inauthenticity—to use an existentialist word— of his normal life.

There is anguish in *The Late Mattia Pascal*. Reflection on his state turns Adriano into a spectator of his own life, and thus prevents him from living. But there is also a degree of optimism, for Adriano-Mattia's decisive choice is a conscious one. When Adriano leaves his hat and walking stick on the bridge across the Tiber in the simulation of his second suicide (the first was an accident), he is no longer running away. With a strong assertion of the will, he turns toward responsibility, intending both to right the wrong he has done as Adriano (permitting a girl to fall in love with his fictional self) and to seek compensation for the wrongs done to him as Mattia. He will return home to his wife and his mother-in-law, no longer to suffer indignities but to rebel against them in some realistic and acceptable fashion. It is not his fault if by a last quirk he is deprived of that satisfaction. In the two years of his absence, his wife, for whom time had *not* stood still, remarried and she is now the mother of a child. Mattia accepts the reality that has been created. He assumes the personality that has been created for him, and in a still new change becomes the living late Mattia Pascal. His old friend and fellow librarian, Don Eligio, may summarize the moral of the tale as follows: "It is impossible to live outside of the law and outside of those peculiarities, sad or happy as they may be, which determine what we are." But it is a conclusion that understandably enough makes no sense for the late Mattia. The lesson *he* has learned is a different one. He has learned it on the eve of his second suicide in an encounter with his shadow, and it is the lesson of compassion. In the hatred that welled up in him at the realization that not he had played a trick on life but life—in the shape of his wife and mother-in-law—had played a trick on him, he had caught sight of his shadow on the pavement and in a fit of rage had raised his foot to trample it:

But no, I . . . I could not stamp upon my shadow. Who was more of a shadow of the two of us? I or it? Two shadows! There, there on the ground; and anyone could step on it, crush my head, crush my heart, and I would keep silent, my shadow would be silent. . . . But yes! That is how it was! that shadow was the symbol, the ghost of my life: it was I, there on the ground, exposed to the mercy of other men's feet. . . . But that shadow had a heart and was unable to love; it had money and anyone could rob it from it; it had a head, but only to think and realize that it was the head of a shadow, and not the shadow of a head. . . . And at that I felt it to be a living thing, and I felt pain for it, as though the horse and the wheels of the wagon and the feet of the passers-by had actually torn it asunder. And I could not leave it there any longer, laid bare there, on the ground.

In this traditional Romantic image of the dissociation of the personality, of the *Doppelgänger*, the personal element, the Pirandello touch, is the revelation of grief. The pain Mattia feels for his objectified self, and the fact that sympathy and

[17]

sorrow have taken the place of hatred and rage, make possible the sublimation, the ascetic overcoming of self, with which the book ends. Mattia's decision to write the story of his strange adventure—that is, the substitution of art for life—clinches his acceptance of his new role as survivor of himself, and places a second reconciliation, a further denial of tragedy, beside the one expressed by Don Eligio. This, I believe, is the chief reason why, in spite of its disconsolate insights into the human condition, in spite of its dwelling on the slippery relativism that regulates man's relations with other men and with himself, in spite of its fascinated staring at the rent in the paper heaven that covers the human marionette and at the flickering light of the little private lanterns that men carry around with them to show the way in the great surrounding darkness, *The Late Mattia Pascal* is not a sad book. The more obvious reason is simply the very considerable space filled with the grotesque and the farcical, from the story of the double illegitimate paternity of Mattia (an episode which Pirandello will later develop in *Liolà*), to the tremendous scenes that enliven Mattia's married life, from the pathetic but ridiculous figure of the ex-piano teacher at Adriano's boardinghouse in Rome, to the wonderful double-talk that takes place at the séances held there. The mixture of seriousness and laughter, however, has generally disturbed readers, and critics beginning with Croce have pointed to what they consider the novel's slightness and objected to its improbability and its lack of humanity. Pirandello remained fond of it, and in 1921 wrote a spirited defense of the rights of phantasy. He compared his critics to zoologists who study man because he is a two-legged animal, but would reject from the species the man who has a wooden leg or a glass eye. And he defended the humanness of his *raisonneurs*, their everlasting questioning and worrying, because "man reasons or is irrational—which comes to the same thing—when he suffers."

By 1921 Pirandello had placed quite a number of suffering reasoners on the stage and had dealt with many others in his narrative works. Since it is impossible to consider all of them, we shall have to be content with pausing briefly on the two novels *The Old and the Young* and *Shoot!* (1915), both of which deserve greater attention than is usually granted them, and move then to the group of plays written up to 1921, many of which are adaptations of earlier stories.

The action of *The Old and the Young* takes place between the Italian parliamentary elections of 1892 and the repression of a socialist-inspired rebellion of Sicilian peasants and workers which occurred in 1894. It thus corresponds to the first period of Pirandello's return from Germany and his initial contacts with literary life in Rome. At that time a financial scandal involved a number of high-placed names, a number of heroes of the Risorgimento. The mood of disgust and dejection which seized those who witnessed the scandal—Pirandello among them —is expressed in a famous page of the novel: "From the skies of Italy, those days, mud was falling . . . mud poured in torrents, and it seemed as though all the sewers of the city had overflowed and the national life of the Third Rome was destined to drown in that turbid, fetid flood of slime. . . . It was the bankruptcy of national honor!"

But the historical dimension is only one aspect of *The Old and the Young*. There are also the single stories of individuals caught up in national events, and of other individuals at the mercy of, and instruments of, the tremendous tensions that govern their complicated family relationships. Though the novel pits two generations against one another, it is not one of the customary representations of lack of mutual comprehension between them, of differences that time can heal. Rather, in Pirandello's world, each man must fight for himself, in order to assert his personality and to make room for its growth amid the invading egotism of his fellow men. "Live and let live" is not a maxim in the physically crowded, economically restricted, socially gregarious environment that Pirandello's fictions reflect. This is a basic fact that must be kept in mind if we wish to understand Pirandello on his own terms: the sudden outburst that most of his characters are driven to is the result of a repression to the limit. What strikes even the most superficial reader of *The Old and the Young* is the tremendous solitude in which everyone lives: Don Ippolito and his philosopher-recluse brother, Cosmo, who "has understood the game" (that is, that we create illusions for ourselves and take them for realities); their sister, Donna Caterina, and her son, Roberto; Roberto's idealistic nephew, Antonio del Re, and the pure, simple-minded old *garibaldino*, Mauro Mortara, whose death is one of the most painfully ironical in literature. And even such active individuals as Don Flaminio Salvo, the capitalist entrepreneur who owns land, banks, and sulphur mines, or Nicoletta Capolino, his mistress, are jealously closed within themselves, completely concentrated upon creating those "conscious fictions," as Pirandello calls them, in which spontaneous and sincere reactions are carefully censored and turned into their opposites—a kind of Machiavellianism that marshals the forces not only of the intellect but also of the sentiments. *The Old and the Young* is a long and difficult book. But while it may have been dismissed as an anachronism at the time of its appearance when the historical novel was deemed to be dead, it can hardly be overlooked today by anyone truly interested in reconstructing Pirandello's thought in its entirety.

Shoot!, or to give it its later title, *The Notebooks of Serafino*

Gubbio, Cameraman, is a totally different work. As a first-person narrative and as the chronicle of a rather exceptional personal experience, it goes back to *The Late Mattia Pascal.* The two novels throw light on one another structurally, for they both move flexibly back and forth instead of proceeding directly from beginning to end. But while *The Late Mattia Pascal*'s essentially circular movement—the beginning and the end meeting in Mattia's decision to write the story of his life—is quite simple, *Shoot!*, being both a story and a stream-of-consciousness commentary on that story, is more complex. The novel is divided into Notebooks, and the same characters appear at different moments and in different settings, creating the kaleidoscopic effect of life which is not structured by any unifying concept. In lieu of such a concept there is Serafino Gubbio's observant eye, that is, both his physical eyes and the lens of the camera through which he films a movie being produced at the Kosmograph Studios. In the final scene, a magnificent concretization of multiple metaphors as well as the culminating action of the plot, the movie plot and the fictional real-life plot merge. The story of which Serafino is a witness is the following: Varia Nestoroff, a fascinating Russian actress, is the typical *belle dame sans merci*, alternately possessed by the need to destroy others and to degrade herself. The Second Notebook, which opens in an idyllic, fairy-story landscape at the "Grandparents' House" where time stands forever still (there is even a fountain whose basin never fills!), tells of Mme Nestoroff's seduction of a young painter, Giorgio Mirelli, the naïve and inexperienced grandson of that family of times gone by. Mirelli's erstwhile tutor, Aldo Nuti, a fatuous young man who is engaged to Mirelli's sister, tries to separate the two, but instead he becomes Mme Nestoroff's next victim. Mirelli commits suicide. All of this preceded the action itself and is discovered by Serafino retrospectively as he becomes

[21]

curious about Mme Nestoroff who, together with her present lover, the Sicilian actor Carlo Ferro, is now working at Kosmograph in a film, *The Woman and the Tiger*. This film is to conclude with a spectacular scene—we are in the midst of the nascent grand-scale movie industry—in which a real tiger will actually be killed in a make-believe jungle where a group of make-believe Englishmen are on a make-believe safari. Nuti, the rejected lover now also an actor, reappears. The rivalry between him and Ferro leads to an exchange of roles which puts Nuti into the camouflaged cage of the tiger for the last scene. Maddened by Mme Nestoroff's ostentatious flirting with Ferro, Nuti shoots not the tiger but her, and is in turn torn to pieces by the beast. Serafino—already at the beginning of the novel described as "a hand that turns the crank"—is frozen with horror, but he continues to film the scene, his hand turning impassively, regulating its movement to suit the action taking place before him. At the end when the tiger is shot and Serafino dragged back from the cage, his grasp on the crank is so strong that he cannot let go: "I did not moan, I did not cry. The terror had silenced my voice forever."

Serafino Gubbio's silence has of course symbolic significance. One of the themes of the novel is the mechanization of modern life: "Man," writes Serafino in his diary, "who was once a poet and deified his own feelings to worship them, has now discarded them as useless and dangerous impediments. Having turned wise and industrious, he has begun to build his new gods in iron and steel and has become their servant and their slave. Long live the machine that mechanizes life!" A passage such as this one is by itself nothing new in Pirandello. A good number of the earliest stories ("Sicilian Limes," "The Wet-Nurse," "Fumes") had already given an ironic interpretation of civilization and progress by setting up those antitheses, rural life–city life, genuineness–artifice, simplicity–confusion, innocence–corruption, which have always carried the same implied and unmistakable value judgment. But in *Shoot!* objective criticism of the machine (I say objective in spite of the fact that such criticism is always the result of a nostalgic look backward) does not lead to its rejection. Serafino is and remains a cameraman, proudly perfecting the minuscule area of craftsmanship that is left to him: "I, dear sir," he says to an idler who questions him, "do not always turn the crank in the same way. Sometimes I do it more rapidly, sometimes more slowly, as the circumstances require it." And then, with a wonderful intuition of the direction that modern consciousness and modern art were to take, Pirandello has him add: "I have no doubt, however, that with time, sir, they will succeed in doing without me." This reduction of man to thing goes much further than Pirandello's original view of man as spider, snail, or mollusk—all living organisms belonging to the animal kingdom on however humble a scale—or of the identification of man with puppet, where the puppet is after all still an image—albeit a rough wooden image—of man. But while the puppet gesticulates, its strings pulled by the God-artist puppeteer who transmits something of himself to it, the camera, moved by a hand that simply goes through a quasi-mechanical action, records without any chance of expressing itself through what it holds fast. We have reached the dehumanization of art—and yet this very point has led A. L. De Castris, the critic who has given the most exciting reading of this novel, to conclude that it mirrors the development of Pirandello's own human sympathy "from relative pity to absolute compassion, from sorrowful commentary to 'inanimate silence' (*silenzio di cosa*) . . . from a human to a 'divine' feeling, from 'narrative' pity to the high and invisible pity of the tragic poet"—that is, that it follows the parabola of Pirandello's fictional representations from Mattia Pascal's pity for his shadow to "Henry IV's" wide-eyed, horrified stare. In the

[23]

Sixth Notebook, after Serafino has listened to Mme Nestoroff's confession, he is seized with disgust at the sight of the rising tide of man's anxious and obscene stupidity:

"Insanity, crime, or foolishness. Things fit for the movies! Here it is: this woman in front of me with her copper-colored hair. And over there, on those six canvases [painted by Mirelli at the time of his love for Mme Nestoroff] the bright, luminous dream of a youth who could not come to terms with life. And now, the woman fallen from that dream, fallen from art into the movies. Come then, get the camera ready! Will there be a drama here? Here is the protagonist. Get set, shoot!"

Dramas to be impassively recorded and suffering reasoners who have pushed to the center of the stage are the two basic insights that made possible Pirandello's rapid production of a wide variety of theatrical compositions. By 1921, when *Six Characters* was staged, he had written and seen performed twenty plays. He had at first turned to the theatre with little enthusiasm, merely contributing a few one-act plays to theatrical ventures sponsored by friends—off-Broadway, so to speak. The first group of productions met with little success. One episode, however, bears mentioning. It concerns *Se non così* (originally written in 1896 with the title *Il nibbio*, and published in 1917 as *La ragione degli altri*), the first three-act play performed in 1915 in a regular commercial theatre. During rehearsals, a clash occurred between the leading lady, Irma Gramatica, and the author because they could not agree on the play's central character. Gramatica insisted it was Elena, the mistress who is forced to give up her child; Pirandello, that it was Livia, the sterile wife who cruelly—but with stringent logic—claims the child for herself. This disagreement, which led Pirandello to preface the printed version of the play with a letter addressed to the protagonist Livia, is an indication of the unconventionality of Pirandello's conception. Just as the tragic character is not necessarily the one who dies at the end of the play (as in *The Vise* [1892]), so the greatest suffering does not necessarily take place outside the pale of respectability —the tragedy of a wife can be more moving than the tragedy of a rejected mistress. But, as Pirandello points out in the preface, it was a view for which the audience was not ready.

The second time Pirandello was drawn to the theatre it was in connection with the efforts being made by a number of fellow Sicilians in Rome to raise the level of dialect productions. Angelo Musco, the great actor, literally forced a play out of Pirandello, who was not particularly in favor of dialect, who was ill-disposed toward the gesticulating, insistent Sicilian who had invaded his study, and who was sick with worry about his son who had just left for the front. But he needed money, and he had been pleased with Musco's rendition of *Sicilian Limes* (Musco played in *Sicilian Limes* in 1915, but the play had already been given in 1910). So he derived *Pensaci, Giacomino!* (1916) from a story by the same name, *Il berretto a sonagli* from "A Wronged Husband" and "Sicilian Honor" (both 1912), and wrote *Liolà* (1916) directly for the stage (but note the relationship with an episode of *The Late Mattia Pascal* already mentioned). This series of productions was extremely successful and Musco was to pride himself forevermore on being the one who had launched "the illustrious Master, the most famous, most controversial and acclaimed playwright in the world."

Though all of Pirandello's Sicilian plays merit attention, we shall have to limit our discussion to *Liolà*, which is in a certain sense his farewell to the island. *Liolà* is set in the countryside near Girgenti, and is spoken in the same dialect that had been the subject of Pirandello's dissertation at Bonn. With the philologist's scientific precision, he makes a point of this, distinguishing in the preface to the bilingual edition (1917) between his use of a pure local vernacular and the hybrid "bourgeois dialect" common in other Sicilian plays. Little in *Liolà* recalls the Sicily that had been the literary landscape of so many of his earlier narrative works. Gone is the oppressiveness of the social environment which had been the subject of *The Outcast* (written 1893). Gone the disgusting intrigues of the petty provincial clerical world dealt with in the series of stories first gathered together under the title *Tonache di Montelusa* (the earliest dates from 1896). Gone the grotesqueness of certain marriage arrangements, possible only in a primitive society, which are portrayed in such stories as "The Merry-Go-Round of Love" (written 1895), "Scialle nero" (1900?), or "Male di luna" (1913). Gone the failure of hope in historical change expressed in *The Old and the Young*. Of *Liolà* Pirandello had written his son: "It will be the comedy of a peasant-poet drunk with the sun, as there are so many in Sicily"; and a month later, in August: "I wrote it in two weeks . . . it was my vacation. It is so joyous that it seems hardly possible that it is mine. . . . It will live long." In his singlehanded resistance to fraud, corruption, and folly, the peasant-poet Liolà is a smiling and light-hearted version of Pirandello's usually less quixotic character. Where so many of the others fail, he succeeds in bringing happiness and meting out justice: to the impotent old miser he gives a son; for the humiliated wife he provides the possibility of having a happy and respected home life; the schemer Tuzza he leaves to reap the fruits of her dishonesty. The Sicily of *Liolà* is Pirandello's contribution to the tradition of the pastoral. Its "golden light" (in Bentley's words), its "pagan life" (in Gramsci's), its idyllic tone were made possible not by Pirandello's closeness to Sicily but by the inner distance he had gained from it—a distance which is also revealed in the songs and choruses that add so much to the lightness of the play, and which, as Russo pointed out, are a mixture of verses of folklore

[26]

origin and verses that imitate the Tuscan *dugentista*, Cecco Angiolieri.

But if Pirandello had gained distance from Sicily, he had not gained it from the "raving Lear" who had first appeared to him in Sicilian garb. Leonardo Sciascia, the critic who has most intimately and intelligently understood the Sicilian component of Pirandello's world, speaks of "a current of dialectics and immanentism present beneath the surface conformism of the Sicilian." Pirandello's central fictional character was at first the village philosopher—or madman—driven by an aspiration for absolutes. But the closer Pirandello moved to this character, the less he saw the external facts of his life, his circumstances, his dress, his identity, and the more he discerned his features, the grimace, the distraught look, the discomposed gesturing, that "lean and hungry" quality that warns of the presence of distress, with the consequent danger of an attack on established values. Eventually the local and historical reality which originally conditioned the character was completely subsumed under a universalized representation of anguish. The progression, however, was gradual, and just as there was in Pirandello no conscious abandoning of narrative in favor of drama, so there was no programmatic stepping from one representational world into another. Rather, a cohesive harmony was at work within each play, suiting character to situation, to setting, to language—but then we would hardly expect this to be otherwise.

By looking at the suffering reasoners that Pirandello had by 1921 set on the stage as a group—forgetting, that is, strict chronology—we can see this shift of emphasis in operation. Rosario Chiarchiaro in *The License* (1919) makes his entrance speaking in dialect and wearing a bizarre costume he has himself devised so as to give concrete expression to the role of bearer of the Evil Eye that public opinion has assigned to him.

[27]

Although the pity he evokes from the one Judge who is above convention (and from the reader) is timeless in nature, the situation is thinkable only in terms of a specific superstition operating in a specific locale. Ciampa in *Il berretto a sonagli* also appears on stage speaking dialect, in a situation created by a particular sexual ethic which has its firm and immovable rules of conduct. Again, the reader's sympathy for his plea of being as against seeming knows no boundaries of time or space, but the elements of the plot do. Angelo Baldovino in *The Pleasure of Honesty* (1917), instead, reveals nothing of his background. He is presented as a failure, but the causes of his failure remain generic, barely hinted at by the family friend who selects him as the husband in name only for a girl who is already, and plans to remain, the mistress of someone else. Called upon to play the role of a respectable man in order to save appearances for his "wife" and her lover, Baldovino, with the wonted intransigence of the Pirandellian *raisonneur*, insists on giving a perfect performance. It soon becomes obvious that the two norms of conduct cannot coexist, that being excludes seeming. Baldovino's behavior exposes the dishonesty and hypocrisy of those who had thought to use him for their own ends. He wins the love of his wife. The final dialogue is the result of an inner transformation which has come about through Baldovino's having actually lived the abstract principle of honesty and having thus proved its superiority as the basis for establishing viable human relationships. The action takes place completely on a psychological level, in the experiencing consciousness of those involved.

It is So! (*If You Think So*) is in many respects not substantially different from *The Pleasure of Honesty*. The small-town gossips who want to find out the truth, that is, the objective, documentable facts of the lives of a family of newcomers in their midst, may be misled—and the audience with them—by an

adumbration of specific historical time and place: the earth-
quake that wiped out the town from which the Ponzas have
come really occurred in 1915, and the extreme pettiness of the
bureaucratic milieu in which Ponza works is unmistakably *fin
de siècle* (again a harried clerk at the mercies of his superiors!).
But just as in *The Pleasure of Honesty*, or in *The Rules of the
Game* (1918) and in *Tutto per bene* (1920), the action has
nothing to do with these circumstances, these external and
transitory forms of life, this fake verisimilitude. Ponza, like
Baldovino, reveals very little of his background. The stage
directions at his first appearance specify that he is dark, thick-
set, dressed completely in black, and with a thick black mous-
tache. He is also clenching and unclenching his hands, speaks
with difficulty and ill-contained violence, and his eyes maintain
a hard, fixed, somber stare. Obviously Pirandello presents him
as wearing the mask of his anguish and not the dress of his
social condition. In his manner and gesture are contained the
outcome—the epilogue—of the drama through which he has
lived. But if like every other Pirandellian character Ponza is
"caught in situation," he is nevertheless used differently by the
author. Unlike Baldovino or "Henry IV" or Martino Lori (in
Tutto per bene, 1920) or Ersilia Drei (in *To Clothe the Naked*,
1922), Ponza does not live through an experience on stage.
True, he comes forth to defend himself, to give his version of
the reason why he keeps his wife and mother-in-law from see-
ing one another. Through Laudisi, Pirandello's spokesman, he
pleads for each man's right to his "phantom" (the illusions men
create about themselves and about one another and in which
they live "in perfect harmony, pacified"). But he does not
change in the course of the play. What he knows at the end he
already knew at the beginning; he has simply suffered more.
And, objectively, as a character created by Pirandello to a certain end, he has served—together with Signora Frola, Laudisi,

[29]

and the veiled woman of the final scene—to demonstrate a truth, to teach a lesson. This separation between the story which is told and the purpose to which it is told will reappear again in *Six Characters*, in *Each in His Own Way* (1924), and in *Tonight We Improvise* (1930). And in these plays, as in *It is So!*, this duality will confuse the issue for the spectator, who is asked to give up his most deeply cherished expectation, that of being told a story and how it ends. But though there is separation between story and purpose in the trilogy of the theatre within the theatre there is no clash between them, for the character plays himself as character in the making—that is, dramatizes himself in his role of character—and the intellectual, discursive content of the play is completely absorbed into the fiction itself. In the parable *It is So!*, instead, the characters are simply themselves, but as in all allegory the spectator is left with the feeling that some violence has been done to them, that they have been manipulated. That is why I am somewhat perplexed by the general enthusiasm for this play. Of course it succeeds in teaching its lesson on the relativity of truth very effectively; the situation through which it does so—which one of two people is the crazy one?—is a set comedy piece; at the end there is even an overt plea for compassion, an appeal to the finer sentiments. But what I miss in *It is So!* is the tremendous and unequivocal pressure of life on stage that we find elsewhere in Pirandello.

Henry IV (1922) gives us this pressure in its fullest tragic impact. Its protagonist is the self-aware and passionate Pirandellian hero caught at the moment of his highest distress. His "phantom" is the most fragile of all, the most self-contained and lonely one, and it is about to be snatched from him. "Henry" does not only *seem* mad to the frivolous, uncompassionate, and uncomprehending crowd that presses—and has always pressed—in upon him, he has actually *been* mad. He has plumbed the abyss of incommunicability when one day "look-ing into a pair of eyes . . . like a beggar before a door he will never be able to enter," he had realized that, even if he were to get in, it would not be as himself with his inner world as he saw and felt it but as a stranger to himself, as the one "the other one [the owner of the pair of eyes] sees and feels in his own impenetrable world." Compassion, which is meaning-ful in the microcosm of *It is So!* where Ponza, his wife, and his mother-in-law support one another by reciprocally creating the life-giving illusion of form, has no place in *Henry IV.* "Henry" is already all form. It is a form no one has given him and no one can share with him, except—supreme irony—the play-actors who are hired to sham his court. These play-actors have an important role in revealing the meaning of the tragedy to the audience. It is they who first introduce "Henry" in a scene which lulls the audience into a false calm. While waiting for the "Emperor" and instructing the latest recruit, the latest "Secret Counselor," in his duties, they step in and out of their roles, triggering that laughter in the spectators which signals the happy recognition that all is as it should be: a wealthy madman may permit him-self the luxury of building a castle for his folly ("Henry" has been living in a fake environment since the day, twenty years before, when he was thrown from his horse during a pageant in which he was wearing the costume of the German Emperor Henry IV), but the men he employs to second that folly have their feet on the ground and enter into the make-believe know-ingly, thus vindicating the eternal superiority of the sane man over the madman. But it is the only comic moment in the play. When "Henry" is mentioned again in the course of the arrange-ments that are made for a "shock treatment" which is supposed to cure him of his delusion and fling him into the present, he bears all the marks not of the madman but of the exceptional individual, the lucid, observant, critical mind that "has under-

[31]

stood the game." Even before the accident, we are told, "Henry" was different: Donna Matilda, with whom he had been in love, speaks of him as "a bit strange . . . fanatical . . . eccentric"; Belcredi, who had then been his rival and is now Matilda's lover, gives a perceptive analysis of his "lucid over-excitement" in which spontaneity and immediate reflection on that spontaneity—living and watching oneself live—appeared to be at constant war with one another. There follows the evocation of the moment after the accident, when the merrymakers suddenly became aware that, while they were play-acting in their roles, "Henry" was in earnest, the *mask* of the Emperor had become his *person:* "I shall never forget that scene, all our made-up faces, so hideous and so vulgar, before the terrible mask of his face, that was no longer a mask, but madness personified!" The audience is thus prepared for the first appearance of Henry IV and for the scene that follows, in which—in a manner of speaking—both Henrys find themselves on stage together. "Henry" *is* Henry IV, and because of this all the others are forced into their supporting roles; but "Henry" is also suspiciously like himself, that is, he "philosophizes" in a manner appropriate both to his fictional self and to his real self (*if* we and Donna Matilda and Belcredi could be absolutely certain that he does have a real self). The scene is the dramatization of the confrontation between sanity and madness that "Henry" later describes to his "Secret Counselors": "Do you know what it means to find yourself face to face with a madman—with someone who shakes the foundations of everything you have built up in yourself and around you, your logic, the logic of all your constructions?"

We have moved then from the initial reassurance that the world of the sane is superior to the world of the insane to the disquieting thought that the unstable, inconstant, and voluble structure that the madman gives the world may invalidate the solid and logical construction of the sane, of the perfect conformist. But if to be watched and judged by the heightened, half-disfiguring, and thereby half-configuring, intelligence of the psychotic is disturbing and unsettling, to be watched and judged by a coolly composed and intentional madness—that is, by the intelligence that has understood the game and can no longer bear to have anything to do with it—is simply unbearable. This is essentially what happens in *Henry IV* when it is revealed that, though "Henry" had been ill for twelve years, he had one day awakened as from a dream and had then decided—rationally decided—to remain fixed in his madness. There is no doubt that this is the high point of the play, the heavy center of Pirandello's tragic message. "Henry" 's tragic insight occurs not at the end, when in a surge of form-shattering life he has killed Belcredi, but it had occurred eight years earlier when he suddenly opened his eyes again: ". . . and I was terrified for I knew at once that it was not only my hair that had turned gray, but that everything had turned gray, that everything had collapsed and was ended. And I would be arriving, with the hunger of a wolf, at a banquet that had already been cleared away." As always in Pirandello the game has already been played out before the action on stage begins, and we are set before an epilogue. What "Henry" had with his superior wisdom and in strong self-renunciation composed is ruthlessly destroyed by the stupid meddling of a doctor more interested in the cure than in the patient, by a vapid, flighty, middle-aged woman in search of sensation, and by that incarnation of evil, Belcredi, the man who originally precipitated the tragedy through one of those idiotic jokes (he had pricked "Henry" 's horse during the cavalcade) that respectable society at all levels—the society of the well adjusted—condones and laughs at. *Henry IV* can be understood properly only if the minor figures too are given full attention, for they stand concretely for all of the gradations in the inability of the average man to accept otherness. "Henry" 's tragedy is not simply that he *is* other, but that he has understood his otherness and that he has found that in the corrupt, egotistic, and foolish world around him there is no place for it. His exclusion is therefore doubly definitive: the sword thrust at the end underscores and fixes forever the intuition of his tremendous aloneness: "This," he had said at one point, showing the costume he was wearing, " . . . is for me the evident, voluntary caricature of that other constant and continuous masquerade of which we are the involuntary clowns, when, without knowing it, we mask ourselves to appear what we think we are."

Henry IV is Pirandello's highest achievement. Its intellectual content is absorbed completely and expressed completely—without leaving any residues—through the representation on stage. It is the play in which the famous "ideas"—though they are all present as in a compendium—intrude the least, and which best shows that all along it was not the mask but the face behind it that concerned Pirandello. Its many-sidedness will continue to elicit critical attention for as long as the experience of man's encounter with nonbeing, with the void, will have any intellectual or emotional resonance.

In *Henry IV* Pirandello gave complete and permanent life to the kind of character he elsewhere portrayed as stillborn. "Henry" has the rich, autonomous being in art which makes him the fixed center of a confluence of meanings, including some, as the Father in *Six Characters* says, never intended by the author. "Henry"—and there are a host of similarly successful characters in Pirandello's works—takes his place beside Francesca, Sancho Panza, and Don Abbondio (to cite only those named by Pirandello himself) as the living character who can even scoff at death because he survives his author who is lowered to the status of mere instrument in his creation.

The focus of attention shifts radically in the three plays that deal directly with the problem of artistic creation. Not existential anguish as such but the anguish of the character in search of being is their subject. Ostensibly they are concerned with the interaction of character, actor, and spectators in the creation of the illusion of life on stage, but it does not take much to see that for Pirandello the theatre is simply a concretization of the concept of artistic form. Of the three, *Six Characters* is deservedly the recognized masterpiece, although the later two make greater use of the total resources of theatre and stage and have thus a special place in the history of the experimental theatre. In *Each in His Own Way* the protagonists of the real-life situation which is being performed as a *comédie à clef* (the story is derived from an episode in *Shoot!*) are present among the public. They have come to watch and criticize the interpretation of their drama, much as the six characters take issue with their stand-ins; but, contrary to what happens in the earlier play, they are so disturbed by what they see that they themselves begin to doubt what their motives had actually been. In the dichotomy of being and seeming, seeming may after all *be* being. *Tonight We Improvise* puts on stage—a stage that spills over into the orchestra pit and even the theatre lobby—a group of actors who have only a scenario to go by (based on Pirandello's 1910 story "Leonora, addio!"). They are at odds with a dictatorial director who expects from them the obedience of marionettes. The action finally erupts with rapid excitement when they are left to their own spontaneous *élan vital*. Both of these plays are important contributions to the statement and expression of Pirandello's ideas, but they lack the basic simplicity of *Six Characters* and add unnecessary complications to the latter's embodiment of Pirandello's view of the relationship between Life and Art.

The invention of *Six Characters*—its story line—is the arrival in a theatre of a strange family that introduces itself as having been thought up by an author who then abandoned the work in which they were to appear. Finding the setting for their interrupted fictional existence ready—that is, finding a stage with all its appurtenances open for use—they demand to be given a chance to exhibit the drama that is in them. This wonderfully whimsical and completely theatrical situation, which at once takes the spectator into the artist's workshop, had been maturing in Pirandello's mind for many years. As early as 1904 he had written to a friend that if his financial cares and social obligations permitted it he would be perfectly happy to sit in his study all day, "at the service of the characters of my stories who crowd about me, each one wanting to come to life before the others, each one with his particular unhappiness to make public." The 1911 story "A Character in Distress" is a development of this theme and a fictional transposition of it into the story of Dr. Fileno, whose rejection by Pirandello foreshadows the rejection of the six characters, and whose eloquent description of the condition of the character will return verbatim in a speech of the Father's. But even more significant is the piece "Colloqui coi personaggi" (1915), which is included among the stories but is more properly described as transposed autobiography. It is a beautiful document of Pirandello's most intimate feelings at the time of the war when, in a kind of magic gesture against destruction, he opened wide the floodgates of life in that pantheistic vision of nature in its eternal renewal, which is after all as fundamental an aspect of his art as is the much decried "cerebralism":

In the darkness that gathered slow and tired at the end of those long sultry summer afternoons . . . I had for the past few days no longer felt alone. There was something teeming in that darkness, in a corner of my room. Shadows in the shadow, that sorrowfully shared my anxiousness, my longing, my disappointments, and my sudden fits—all of my feelings, from which they had perhaps been born or were just beginning to be born. They looked at me, they watched me. They would look at me until finally, against my will, I would be forced to turn to them. With whom could I communicate at a moment like that, except with them? And I approached that corner and forced myself to look at them one by one, those shadows born of my passion, and I began to speak with them quietly.

Both the Father and the Daughter refer to just such a moment in their effort to convince the director that their unwritten drama is more worthy of performance than *The Rules of the Game* which is being rehearsed. As a matter of fact, they live this moment on stage, treating the director as they would the author. This of course shows up the director who is indeed a poor substitute for the author, a mere secretary who can only write under dictation, a "translator" who interprets but cannot create. As a consequence, the characters' aspiration to life is again blocked and the work remains unfinished. They leave the stage unrealized, their shadows projected against the backdrop, each in its characteristic stylized and eternal gesture. The two children, however, who in the course of the action had been represented as dead, are not with them.

This last touch in Pirandello's invention invites a further consideration. The plot—if it can be called so—we have just outlined is of the utmost simplicity: the characters are set on stage and after a while they are taken off again. There is, however, a complementary story being told. There are the characters but there is also the content of their lives. Here we encounter Pirandello's familiar social nihilism. The Father is an eccentric who applies the yardstick of his rationalism to life. Having noticed that there was greater compatibility between his wife and a secretary of his than between his wife and himself, he had made it possible for the two to leave together and to set up their own—though illegitimate—family. When the

[37]

second "husband" dies, the wife, now nothing but a mother, is forced to eke out a meager living by working for a dressmaker who is a madam on the side. The Father, having lost sight of his wife's second family, comes to Mme Pace's establishment and there meets his stepdaughter. The Mother arrives to separate them, and the Father, horrified by what has just happened, reunites the whole family (there was a son from the original marriage) in his house. The tensions that result from the cohabitation of the two families—the destructive resentment of the Daughter, the icy disdain of the Son, the Father's sense of guilt, and the Mother's grief—lead to the tragic death of the two children. The girl accidentally drowns in a pool in the garden, the boy shoots himself. The two scenes which the characters act out are the scene at Mme Pace's and the scene in the garden. There is squabbling at each: the characters insist on absolute verisimilitude, the director thinks of the conventional form the play must take, the actors instinctively translate the characters' experience into set pieces of a repertoire of types. All of this creates comic situations by holding the mirror up not to life but to life as it is reflected in art. At the same time there is the serious note of the characters' drama as a real-life situation. Critics usually call this drama melodramatic and sensational and dismiss it as such; I think, however, that not in its details but in the emotions that it releases it is not any more melodramatic and sensational than are love and hate, and the straining between the two. After all it is precisely in the Preface to *Six Characters* that Pirandello gives the definition of his art as transcending representationalism, as having a "philosophical" meaning.

But there is another and yet stronger source of pathos in *Six Characters*: the Father's crying out for the certainty that only history and art can give. "Il piacere della storia" (the pleasure of history), "Henry" had called it when he had described it to his "counselors": "Fixed forever, you could rest in it, admiring how every effect follows obediently upon its cause with perfect logic, and every event takes place precisely and coherently in each of its particulars." This is the structure, the meaning, that man seeks in his own life, and it is not by accident that Pirandello has the simple-minded, hired "counselors" recognize it as such and exclaim over its beauty. For in *Six Characters* Pirandello's intuition is not only, as Fergusson puts it so well, that there is an analogy between his problem as an artist and the problem of the characters who are also seeking form and meaning, but that there is a further analogy between the quest of the tormented character and the desire of all men to know their destiny once and for all, to rest in their meaning. There are thus not only two levels in the play but three, with the two stories, the two plots, both lighting up the ultimate, most abstract, and universal concept, that of life in search of its authentic form. The Father's distress is both the guilt he feels because of the circumstances of the story he acts out—his drama—and the anguish he feels as an unfinished character. There is no separation between these two realities of his, as there is no separation between the double reality of the children, walk-ons who have no speech as far as the theatre is concerned, but persons who have a fate as far as life is concerned. "Fiction? Reality? Fiction! Reality!" are the words that actors and characters are left shouting at one another when the Boy's gun is turned upon himself. And because the spectator is left with that same doubt—which the last brilliant theatrical device of omitting the children's shadows from the final procession underscores—this which could have been but another fictional treatment of the problem of the artist becomes instead a complex many-layered metaphor of the human condition.

Slightly more than half of Pirandello's theatrical production postdates *Six Characters* and *Henry IV*. But three of the later plays still belong in chronology and achievement to the season of the masterpieces: *At the Exit* (1922, but first published in 1916), *To Clothe the Naked* (1922), and *The Man with the Flower in His Mouth* (1923). *To Clothe the Naked* is Pirandello's most directly human work. Gone is the awe that surrounds the figure of "Henry"; gone the admiration for genial theatricality that *Six Characters* calls forth. Ersilia Drei, the protagonist of *To Clothe the Naked*, is only a poor little governess, victimized and without hope to the point that she attempts suicide. At the hospital, near death, she is interviewed by an enterprising journalist, Pirandello's familiar meddler now justified by his profession. He manages to "do a piece" that evokes so much sympathy for her that a well-known novelist is inspired to write her story, her ex-fiancé breaks up his current engagement to hasten to her side, and the man from whose house she has been dismissed comes to Rome to demand a retraction of the article which had placed his family in a bad light. It is, one might say, a situation rich in comic possibilities, and that Pirandello recognizes it as such is made explicit at one point when the novelist tells his vulgar, sentimental, and moralistic landlady that, if he were to include *her* in his story, it would indeed turn into a comedy. But as the action unfolds it becomes obvious that in spite of the bourgeois setting—one of the best in all Pirandello—and in spite of the presence of a few stock characters from the comic repertoire, this is far from being a comedy, even of the genre of the *comédie larmoyante*. For on a purely psychological level Ersilia's encounter with nonbeing, with the void, is not dissimilar from "Henry" 's. But being a humble and not a regal figure she must really die, not just die to ordinary life, in order to be permitted to have her form, to have not the mantle of an emperor but her "decent little dress." And further, being not an intellectual like "Henry" but only a bit of suffering humanity, she is able to do what he could not nor did not need to do—forgive those who persecuted her by recognizing that they too need to construct themselves, that they too wish to cover their ugliness with a beautiful dress. Rarely has Pirandello's exposure of egotism been so merciless. Relentlessly Ersilia is pushed out, excluded, until there is nothing left for her to do but repeat the act of suicide. *To Clothe the Naked* is, I believe, the indispensable complement to *Henry IV*. The two plays illumine one another in more ways than one, but, most significantly, *To Clothe the Naked* offers a clue as to why Pirandello considered *Henry IV* a tragedy: it is in fact the only one of his plays that has in the hero's condition (though it is an assumed one) and in his predicament the necessary requisites of that genre.

The two one-acters, *At the Exit* and *The Man with the Flower in His Mouth,* reveal a secondary but important aspect of Pirandello which we have so far neglected. The first is a dialogue between apparitions, "a profane mystery" Pirandello called it, a calm surrealistic dream sequence which represents death as the slow cessation of all desires. The figure of a little boy whose shadow persists just long enough to eat the pomegranate he had wished for before dying is particularly beautiful and poetic. In *The Man with the Flower in His Mouth* attachment to life in a man whose death from cancer is imminent is also expressed in an epiphany of insignificant things that by their very ordinariness, by their mere existing, provide the necessary anchor to life. The famous passage in which the man evokes shop clerks lovingly attentive to the minutest detail of making a package is a masterful example of that heightening of reality characteristic of surrealism, which here bears no traces of deformation or grotesqueness. Both of these plays show in the complete depersonalization of their characters the turning of all historically rooted conditions into symbol.

[41]

This orientation is also at the basis of Pirandello's three "myths," *The New Colony* (1928), *Lazarus* (1929), and *The Mountain Giants* (1937), of the fairy-tale–legend, *La favola del figlio cambiato* (1934), and of the phantasy, *I'm Dreaming, but Am I?* (1931, but first published in 1929). Although left unfinished at Pirandello's death, *The Mountain Giants* is the best known of these plays and has often been performed. Its themes take us back to *Six Characters*, but the frame of reference is no longer the individual whose experience is universalized but society itself. The remains of a company of actors has been wandering through the countryside seeking an audience for a play that no one appreciates. The poet who wrote the play had committed suicide because the prima donna of the company had refused his love, and now in an ever-repeated act of reparation she seeks to give to the work the life she had taken from its author. The company arrives one night at an abandoned villa high in the mountains, where a strange group of people has taken refuge, led by the magician Crotone. The villa is the realm of phantasy: "We are here at the edges of life," says Crotone. "At a simple command barriers fall. The invisible appears. Phantasms emerge out of the air. . . . I make happen what otherwise happens only in dreams." And in fact, in an eery and beautiful scene thoughts, dreams, and wishes materialize, and each member of the company discovers that he is both the body asleep in bed and the "spirit" abroad in the magic of the night. Crotone invites the actors to give up their useless quest and to share with him and his companions the absolute freedom of living in the imagination alone: "Here we are outside the limits of the natural and the possible. . . . For us it is enough to imagine something and it comes to life by itself." But the actors are incapable of understanding what is being offered them. They insist on *performing* their phantasy world; that is, they are unable to sacrifice their own personalities and the sense of their indispensability to the work of art, to the created thing itself. So they issue forth again and bring their play to the wedding festivities of the "Giants," a race of exceptional men completely absorbed in the cares of the practical world, in exploiting the natural resources of the mountain where they live for the ends of material progress. The play, Pirandello's own *La favola del figlio cambiato*, has no meaning to the revelers, and in a drunken frenzy the leading lady and the two actors who really believe in her mission are savagely attacked and mauled to death. In spite of its fragmentary state (the last act is missing) *The Mountain Giants* is in parts powerful theatre. And in the figure of Crotone Pirandello has created another projection of himself as the self-effacing artist completely tensed to the perception of the abundant life that swirls about him. But it is now no longer simply case histories that are told him, no longer simply characters that burst in upon him. What he receives knowledge of now are "other beings of which men in their normal state have no perception," the nonhuman inhabitants of the world, the spirits of nature that live in the rocks and the woods, in the fire and in the air. In other words, we are back at the very origins of art and—by that fact itself—of religion.

The manifestations of the unconscious had always had an important part in Pirandello's work, though sometimes—as in "The Haunted House" (1905) or in the séance sequence of *The Late Mattia Pascal*—they had appeared in the more primitive form of the supernatural. In the stories of his last period, instead, the unconscious is taken purely and simply as a psychological or metaphysical dimension, not a force to be controlled but an instrument and a source of knowledge. These stories, like the plays we have just mentioned, are dreams, or myths, or allegories. In "Soffio" (1931), for instance, the protagonist discovers that he has the power of life and death over other men,

[43]

and step by step he comes to realize that he himself is Death. In "Cinci" (1932) a boy kills another one, and then forgets about it as though not he but someone else in him had committed the murder. In "Il chiodo" (1936) another boy also kills—in a completely absurd act—simply because he had found a nail on the street and the nail "had wanted" to be used. "Di sera, un geranio" (1934) takes up the mood of *At the Exit* again and evokes the evanescence of consciousness that accompanies death. And finally, in "A Day Goes By" (1936), it is Pirandello himself who takes leave of life (he died a year later, in 1937), in an allegorical vision that equates the whole course of a man's existence to the length of a day beginning in the predawn darkness and ending in the same darkness seventy years later. It is impossible to speak briefly of stories such as these, for each one invites in its fusion of image and meaning the long and patient attention which is usually granted only to poetry.

This is the very attention that Pirandello's work has by and large been denied. And yet, when the "philosophical" interpretations became increasingly the fashion in the twenties, Pirandello himself more than once pointed to what the more balanced view should be: "My works are born of living images, the inexhaustible and perennial source of art. . . . A work of mine is never a concept which seeks expression through images, but an image . . . that, feeding on the intellectual efforts of the mind, by itself takes on a universal meaning through the intimate coherence of art alone." It should come as no surprise that the key to Pirandello's poetic universe is thus ultimately in the images that held meaning for him—the stage being itself but one of those images. The dramatic concepts and the theatrical devices which he popularized and often invented made of him a major determining force in the modern theatre. But by virtue of his total *œuvre* he belongs among the prime poetic imaginations of that late-nineteenth-century–early-twentieth-century transition period that witnessed the cruel and tragic disintegration of values from which modern man has not yet recovered. As for the commitment of the artist to his work, Pirandello is an example of well-nigh total dedication to the intuited embryonic life that seeks liberation through the gift of artistic form.

SELECTED BIBLIOGRAPHY

NOTE: *There is no critical edition of Pirandello's works. In the Omnibus edition of* Novelle per un anno *(2 vols., Milan, Mondadori, 1937–38) an effort was made to give variants and changes as indicated by Pirandello himself, but the revision stopped midway in the material at hand. On this problem, as well as for the most nearly complete list of translations of the short stories in English, see Luigi Pirandello,* Short Stories, *selected, translated, and introduced by Frederick May (London, Oxford University Press, 1965, pp. 237–51). The standard edition of Pirandello is the so-called* edizione definitiva, *published by Mondadori in Milan. It consists of six volumes as listed below.*

PRINCIPAL WORKS OF LUIGI PIRANDELLO

Novelle per un anno. Ed. Corrado Alvaro. 2 vols. 1956–57.
Tutti i romanzi. Ed. Corrado Alvaro. 1957.
Maschere nude. Ed. Silvio d'Amico. 2 vols. 1958.
Saggi, poesie, scritti vari. Ed. Manlio Lo Vecchio-Musti. 1960. Includes an extensive bibliography, covering also Pirandello in translation.

PRINCIPAL TRANSLATIONS OF PIRANDELLO'S WORKS

Novels

The Outcast (L'esclusa). Tr. Leo Ongley. New York, Dutton, 1925.
The Late Mattia Pascal (Il fu Mattia Pascal). Tr. Arthur Livingston. New York, Dutton, 1923. Also tr. William Weaver. New York, Doubleday, 1964.
The Old and the Young (I vecchi e i giovani). Tr. C. K. Scott-Moncrieff. 2 vols. New York, Dutton, 1928.
Shoot! (Si gira). Tr. C. K. Scott-Moncrieff. New York, Dutton, 1926.
One, None and a Hundred Thousand (Uno, nessuno e centomila). Tr. Samuel Putman. New York, Dutton, 1933.

Short Stories

Short Stories. Selected, translated, and introduced by Frederick May. London, Oxford University Press, 1965.
The Merry-Go-Round of Love and Selected Stories (Il turno). Tr. Frances Keene and Lily Duplaix. Foreword by Irving Howe.

New York, The New American Library, 1964. (A Signet Classic.)
Short Stories. Tr. Lily Duplaix. Introduction by Frances Keene. New York, Simon and Schuster, 1959.

Plays
Naked Masks. Ed. Eric Bentley. New York, Dutton, 1958.
The Mountain Giants and Other Plays. Translated and introduced by Marta Abba. New York, Crown Publishers, 1958.
The Rules of the Game. Ed. E. Martin Browne. Penguin Books, 1959.
To Clothe the Naked and Two Other Plays. Tr. William Murray. New York, Dutton, 1962.
Pirandello's One-Act Plays. Tr. William Murray. New York, Doubleday Anchor Books, 1964.
Samuel French Inc., New York, has published the following plays translated by Marta Abba: To Find Oneself (Trovarsi), 1943; As You Desire Me (Come tu mi vuoi), 1948; No One Knows How (Non si sa come), 1949; The Wives' Friend (L'amica della mogli), 1949; Diana and Tuda (Diana e la Tuda), 1950; Tonight We Improvise (Questa sera si recita a soggetto), 1960.

Essays and Critical Writings
"On Humor." Excerpts from L'umorismo. Tr. Teresa Novel. *Tulane Drama Review*, T31 (Spring, 1966), 46–59.
"Theatre and Literature." Tr. A. M. Webb. In Block and Salinger, eds., The Creative Vision, pp. 106–12. New York, Grove Press, 1960.
"The New Theatre and the Old." Tr. Herbert Goldstone. In Block and Salinger, eds., The Creative Vision, pp. 113–30. New York, Grove Press, 1960.
"The Poetry of Dante." Tr. Gian Paolo Biasin. In John Freccero, ed., Dante: A Collection of Critical Essays, pp. 14–22. Englewood Cliffs, N.J., Prentice-Hall, 1965.
"Pirandello on Verga." Tr. Olga Ragusa. In O. Ragusa, Verga's Milanese Tales, pp. 106–26. New York, S. F. Vanni, 1964.
"Tendencies of the Modern Novel," *Italian Quarterly*, VI, No. 23–24 (Fall–Winter, 1962), 36–45. Reprinted from *Fortnightly Review*, Vol. CXXXV (April, 1934).

CRITICAL WORKS AND COMMENTARY

Barilli, Renato. "La poetica di Pirandello" and "Le novelle di

Pirandello," in La barriera del naturalismo, pp. 9–59. Milan, Mursia, 1964.

Bentley, Eric. "Il Tragico Imperatore," *Tulane Drama Review*, T31 (Spring, 1966), 60–75.

Blanquat, J. "D'une jarre à un moulin à vent," *Revue de littérature comparée*, XV (1966), 294–302.

Büdel, Oscar. Pirandello. New York, Hillary House Publishers Ltd., 1966.

Cambon, Glauco, ed. Pirandello: A Collection of Critical Essays. Englewood Cliffs, N.J., Prentice-Hall, 1967.

De Castris, A. L. Storia di Pirandello. Bari, Laterza, 1962.

Di Pietro, Antonio. Saggio su Luigi Pirandello. Saggi e Ricerche, Vol. I. Milan, Università Cattolica del Sacro Cuore, 1941.

Fergusson, Francis. "Action as Theatrical: Six Characters in Search of an Author," in The Idea of a Theatre. Princeton, Princeton University Press, 1949. (Paperback edition, Doubleday Anchor Books, 1953, pp. 196–205.)

Ferrante, Luigi. Pirandello. Florence, Parenti, 1958.

Giudice, Gaspare. Luigi Pirandello. Turin, U.T.E.T., 1963.

Janner, Arminio. Luigi Pirandello. Florence, La Nuova Italia, 1948.

Modern Drama, Vol. VI (1964).

Poggioli, Renato. "Pirandello in Retrospect," in The Spirit of the Letter, pp. 146–70. Cambridge, Mass., Harvard University Press, 1965.

Rauhut, Franz. Der junge Pirandello oder das Werden eines existentiellen Geistes. Munich, C. H. Beck, 1964.

Sciascia, Leonardo. Pirandello e il pirandellismo. Caltanissetta, Salvatore Sciascia, 1953.

——— "Pirandello," in Pirandello e la Sicilia, pp. 9–124. Caltanissetta, Salvatore Sciascia, 1961.

Whitfield, J. H. "Pirandello and T. S. Eliot: An Essay in Counterpoint," *English Miscellany*, IX (1958), 329–57.

——— A Short History of Italian Literature, pp. 278–88. Penguin Books, 1960.